AN IDEAS INTO ACTION GUIDEBOOK

Leadership Coaching

When It's Right and When You're Ready

IDEAS INTO ACTION GUIDEBOOKS

Aimed at managers and executives who are concerned with their own and others' development, each guidebook in this series gives specific advice on how to complete a developmental task or solve a leadership problem.

LEAD CONTRIBUTOR	Douglas Riddle
CONTRIBUTORS	Al Calarco
	Candice Frankovelgia
	Gina Hernez-Broome
	Bev Paulin
	Clemson Turregano

DIRECTOR OF PUBLICATIONS	Martin Wilcox
EDITOR	Peter Scisco
ASSOCIATE EDITOR	Karen Lewis
DESIGN AND LAYOUT	Joanne Ferguson
CONTRIBUTING ARTISTS	Laura J. Gibson
	Chris Wilson, 29 & Company

CCL No. 441
ISBN No. 978-1-60491-043-8

CENTER FOR CREATIVE LEADERSHIP
WWW.CCL.ORG

AN IDEAS INTO ACTION GUIDEBOOK

Leadership Coaching

When It's Right and When You're Ready

Douglas Riddle

Center for
Creative
Leadership®

THE IDEAS INTO ACTION GUIDEBOOK SERIES

This series of guidebooks draws on the practical knowledge that the Center for Creative Leadership (CCL®) has generated, since its inception in 1970, through its research and educational activity conducted in partnership with hundreds of thousands of managers and executives. Much of this knowledge is shared—in a way that is distinct from the typical university department, professional association, or consultancy. CCL is not simply a collection of individual experts, although the individual credentials of its staff are impressive; rather it is a community, with its members holding certain principles in common and working together to understand and generate practical responses to today's leadership and organizational challenges.

The purpose of the series is to provide managers with specific advice on how to complete a developmental task or solve a leadership challenge. In doing that, the series carries out CCL's mission to advance the understanding, practice, and development of leadership for the benefit of society worldwide. We think you will find the Ideas Into Action Guidebooks an important addition to your leadership toolkit.

Table of Contents

EXECUTIVE BRIEF

Leadership in the top management ranks is often an isolated business. Many managers recognize that to focus their personal development plans they need the uninterrupted time and attention of a skilled, objective facilitator. This guidebook is for managers who are considering leadership coaching as a tool in their personal leadership development. It describes what leadership coaching is and can help you decide whether it is appropriate for your situation. You'll also learn how to locate and select a qualified coach with the professional and personal credentials and characteristics that match your development needs so that you can achieve the goals you've set.

What Is Leadership Coaching?

Leadership coaching is a formal engagement in which a qualified coach works with an organizational leader in a series of dynamic, private sessions designed to establish and achieve clear goals that will result in improved business effectiveness for the individual, as well as his or her team and organization. A good coach helps leaders develop clarity of purpose and focus on action.

Leadership coaching uses the relationship between the coach and the person being coached as a platform for questioning assumptions, stimulating reflection, creating alternatives, and growing perspectives. The coach can be a coach by profession or a leader who uses coaching skills; either way, leadership coaching is consciously and explicitly directed at improving the individual's leadership capacity while achieving organizational objectives. While sometimes aimed at remedying a gap or correcting a fault, it is often focused on readying a leader for increased responsibilities, speeding acclimation to a new challenge, or providing an objective sounding board and thought partner when everyone else around a leader is pushing a viewpoint. This is not to say that personal matters are never included in the coaching work—a leader brings his or her whole life to bear on the leadership task—but it means that the focus of attention is on achieving organizational success.

Is It Right for You Now?

Leadership coaching is a particularly powerful method for learning and change when it is used in the right circumstances and when appropriate lessons are sought. It is not the right solution for every kind of growth or development, but there are situations that seem ideally suited to this approach. To determine whether this is the right action for you to take at this time, think about your context and circumstances. You may be a successful leader who wants to set new goals as a function of continuous development. Other appropriate circumstances include increased complexity, organizational expectations, demands for behavior change, significant transitions, predicted changes, highly politicized environments, and moves from a tactical to a strategic role.

While many challenges are well suited for interventions involving leadership coaching, others clearly are not. Leadership coaching can be overkill when there are simpler, less expensive means of achieving desired results. Under the wrong circumstances, leadership coaching may not be particularly effective. The task is to identify the situations and opportunities that lend themselves most readily to this work.

The following examples are not meant to be exhaustive but to suggest that some kinds of growth opportunities are particularly amenable to success through the involvement of a leadership coach. Each benefits from the human capacity to use relationships for emotional and intellectual support.

The task is to identify the situations and opportunities that lend themselves most readily to this work.

Increased Complexity

If you are conscious of the expanding demands of complexity in your leadership challenges, leadership coaching may be the right step for you. Are you in charge of multiple functions that may or may not be related logically to each other? Directors are often

8

responsible for both client-facing and operational elements of their enterprises, for example. If you're asked whether you are responsible for managing people, managing processes, or managing projects, the answer to all three questions could very well be yes.

Complexity is also increased substantially by the expanding global footprint of many organizations. You may find that you have direct and indirect reports who speak different languages, live in widely dispersed geographies, and come from many cultural backgrounds. You may have to regularly conduct virtual meetings with participants who hold very different ideas about what constitutes courteous conversation and professional modes of communication, what makes for success, and what is the proper stance for leaders to take. This level of complexity is difficult for anyone to manage without the opportunity to discuss the dilemmas and work through solutions in a safe place. Leadership coaching is ideal for this kind of challenge because it gives you the opportunity to develop more effective approaches over time through iterative trials, refining practice and communications repeatedly.

You do not need a global team to experience significant complexity. Times of market chaos and episodes of enterprise or group reorganization test any leader's capacity for flexibility, realistic appraisal of the situation, and search for paths through the storms. Additionally, changing circumstances in your personal life can have significant impact on organizational leadership because of their distraction and the persistent intrusion of emotionally powerful thoughts. These circumstances include personal problems, of course, but even very positive personal situations (marriage, birth of a child, move to a new residence) can make it difficult to keep personal and organizational life in separate focus. The relationship with a leadership coach can help you keep the focus in the right place in the moment, creating structure to permit addressing all the demands you are facing.

Organizational Expectations

Leadership coaching may be the favored developmental methodology for leaders at a certain level in the organization or because the organization is growing a coaching culture. In these beneficial circumstances, you are wise to take advantage of the opportunity. When the organization is willing to provide leadership coaching, those individuals who embrace the opportunity position themselves as ready for advancement and prepared for handling future challenges. Even if your initial impression is that coaching is not for you, it may be worth reconsidering if there is organizational support for this mode of development.

Demands for Behavior Change

A truism of leadership roles is that other people want you to be different and that nearly everyone has an idea of how you should change. Some of the time, the need to operate differently is driven by others who genuinely want you to be more effective. This can be your direct reports, your colleagues in various roles, and your boss. The question is whether you're still hearing the same concerns raised about elements of your leadership behavior or organizational roles that you've heard in the past. If brand-new issues are being raised about behaviors that may be inhibiting your effectiveness, it's possible you can deal with them yourself, without the assistance of a professional coach. If, however, you find the themes or concerns raised are the same as they were last year or ten years ago, your success in understanding and responding to the need for change has likely been limited by the absence of an effective, objective navigator. Think about acquiring a coach to help stimulate new approaches and new answers.

None of us can be objective about our own behavior, and few of us have the emotional distance needed to really understand the viewpoint of others who are affected by our limitations. The key challenge for the leader wanting to improve is the limited useful-ness of the ways people ask for change. Every observer has a piece of the desired improvement, but an idiosyncratic way of describing the need because it comes from his or her individual needs. Often it is difficult to turn what others ask for into reasonable actions. Some-times the feedback from different people is so different as to seem to require completely contradictory actions.

Considerable unnecessary effort is frequently expended as leaders who want to be responsive to legitimate concerns attempt to change themselves in unnatural or ineffective ways. Often, what they react to is not what the speakers intended or even knew they were saying. A well-trained, experienced leadership coach under-stands that verbal descriptions of behavior from others often do not translate directly into changes. Your coach can lead you into explor-ing dimensions of behavior that are not obvious and toward trying changes that have known impact. If you have received feedback that you, for example, have favorites or have difficulty getting everyone on board or need to communicate a more compelling vision, your coach can help you work through the data to understand what is driving the perception. The coach can help you make the changes that are likely to make a difference.

Significant Transitions

Change is part of life, and people generally handle change without too much difficulty. If the number of unknowns exceeds the number of known factors in a new situation, leadership coach-ing may be just what is needed. It can spell the difference between a prolonged period of flailing about and a confident, focused move into a new situation.

Some transitions are especially challenging or have a high level of risk; they require special preparation because so much is at stake. The move to a much larger scope of responsibility, for example, may mean that many more people are dependent on your success for their jobs and futures. It may also mean that established behaviors that helped create success in the past may not be as effective in a new role with different demands. Moreover, prior sources of stability and resources for guidance may not be available. Perhaps you've moved to a new location or your old helpers are simply unfamiliar with the demands of the new work. In a new position, you have not had time to develop the resources of sound thinkers and wise advisors. A professional coach can be that kind of resource.

> Leadership coaching can spell the difference between a prolonged period of flailing about and a confident, focused move into a new situation.

Included in the transitions that may benefit from leadership coaching are new jobs, new bosses, and new limitations, due to problems with health, life circumstances, or the experience of a disability. Each of these requires that you continue managing the leadership responsibility you have while simultaneously mastering the challenges of the added changes. Especially challenging are circumstances where you are geographically far from those who are your emotional support or figures of wisdom you've relied on. Where do your innovating ideas come from? If you've typically come up with your brilliant insights in conversation with special friends, mentors, or colleagues who are no longer near, leadership coaching can provide the right climate for developing new habits of innovation. Similarly, do you have opportunities for reflection so you can keep an awareness of the big picture? Such opportunities are a common casualty of major transitions, and time with a coach can create that platform—a safe, intimate, yet challenging and powerful space for deep thinking and practical reflection. These qualities are not options for effective leaders, but the sources of creativity and the drivers of success.

Predicted Changes

Even when change has been planned for and is part of a larger scheme of development, there can be stages that would benefit from leadership coaching. An ideal example is a planned advancement or promotion. In this case, a comprehensive assessment of readiness and working to prepare can be a big boost for you and your organization. Compressed learning time can lead to a smooth transition; improved confidence of customers, the workforce, and the board; and substantial cost savings.

Some planned changes raise a high degree of ambivalence in all involved, such as the retirement of a key leader in the organization, who may control critical intelligence about the business that has not been completely shared. If you are in such a position, you may have given scant attention to the consequences of stepping out of the limelight or how you will relate to the new leadership. You and your organization may agree that the time is right and the change is necessary, but the sensitivities associated with making the transition can be particularly difficult in the typical absence of a systematic plan for addressing the multiple issues involved. A leadership coach can help you address both your impending personal and professional changes and your obligations to the organization to ensure a healthy future. The coach may also help you determine the personal and organizational legacy that you want to leave within the organization. In some cases the coach will guide both you and the rest of the leadership group in surfacing the important concerns and ensuring they are dealt with in a productive and mutually beneficial way. Similar factors are raised when the event affecting the organization is a planned merger or acquisition. Leadership coaching can be a critical success factor for the individuals involved and for the groups who have to incorporate the changes.

Highly Politicized Environments

Many organizations are full of open or hidden conflict. Repeated mergers or acquisitions or inconsistent or often-changed leadership can result in large groups of constituents feeling demoralized. We are all aware of acquired companies and the survivors of mergers who have been poorly integrated into the new organization. Similar dynamics can be present when a promotion has been handled poorly and former competitors for the key leadership role are required to work together with changed interpersonal and authority dynamics. Leadership coaching introduces the objectivity and balance that allows the creation of so-called third options to reduce the either-or thinking that exacerbates the distress. If you as a leader are faced with complex interpersonal and group dynamics that are the result of historical processes, the persistence and creativity you need to survive and master these situations can be hard to come by. It is easy to be swept up in the prevailing mood or to be swayed by the intensity of perspectives and viewpoints from the long-term conflict. A true thought partner who can hold you accountable and is not beholden to anyone but you can change the odds for your success. This kind of coaching partnership can make an enormous difference in your confidence and reduce the reactivity that conflicted environments thrive on.

Moves from Tactical to Strategic Roles

Leadership coaching really shines in accelerating the acquisition of new perspectives and the implementation of conceptual advances. As a result of the challenging dialogue with a leadership coach, your viewpoint and frame of reference can expand rapidly. You begin to see new things and to see old things in new ways. This is the essence of strategic thinking: the ability to see from multiple flexible perspectives and to get the largest possible frame of reference.

Your leadership coach should push you to go further in your inquiry than you might go alone. Coaching will stretch you to

Other Developmental Resources

Leadership coaching is a remarkably flexible and effective tool for change and growth. It is often most effective when combined with other learning strategies. Consider supplementing your coaching experience with the following resources.

- leadership development programs
- mentoring
- feedback about your impact on your organization and the people in it
- work assignments that provide adequate stretch
- colleagues who share your commitment to advancement and growth
- psychotherapy to address problems whose impact is outside work

consider viewpoints that are not in your normal repertoire. The result is that the questions you ask in meetings, the observations you make, and the guidance you provide others will demonstrate the qualities of strategic thinking and learning that high-performance organizations depend on.

This dynamic is also beneficial for the leader who needs to navigate the political minefields of every large organization. Leadership coaching allows you to question your assumptions and to think through the consequences of your choices in a conversation with another.

What to Expect

Every coaching engagement is unique because of the personal situation of the person and the approach of the coach, but there are key elements that are dependable components of the coaching experience. These consistent elements include setting up the coaching engagement, using assessments, creating action plans and coaching meetings, measuring results, and completing the coaching engagement.

Setting Up the Coaching Engagement

Contracting is the term used for everything involved in setting up the coaching relationship. This refers to much more than contractual aspects, including all the agreements required to set up the coaching relationship in a healthy and productive way. It includes logistical arrangements such as when and how often to meet, what kind of meetings (face to face, telephone, or other virtual modes), and how to handle scheduling and appointment changes. If you are paying for coaching yourself or from your department's budget, agreeing on the fees and determining how missed appointments are handled would be an element of contracting.

Boundaries. One key component to be discussed at the beginning of coaching is the boundaries associated with the coaching relationship. Boundaries include such elements as how information is handled (confidentiality and reporting expectations) and how the coaching relationship fits into the existing network of relationships. It is common practice that some of the information shared with your coach is confidential, but at present there are no legal protections for confidentiality, as there are with a lawyer-client relationship, for example. If you and your coach agree that the specifics of what you discuss are to be kept private while the goals or results of the coaching work can be reported, you can operate under that agreement. The reports that your coach makes to your boss or other organizational representative can be limited to information that can be aggregated across a number of people. Such information might include the themes that persons in coaching relationships have introduced or measurements of satisfaction and the value of the coaching work. At the same time, your coach may support you in the preparation of reports you may want to make to your boss or other stakeholders. These practices seem to facilitate the development of a safe and productive coaching engagement, while keeping your relationship with your boss central.

Organizational expectations. Before the coaching engagement begins, the coach should have reached agreements with the contracting organization about what information will be confidential and provided some guidance to the human resources professionals as well as line managers. However, that does not reduce the need to get similar agreements with your boss and your HR manager. It's frustrating when your boss asks for a written report from your coach six months into the engagement and you have to deal with the ensuing confusion and disappointment. This illuminates the importance of the "boss alignment meeting" early in the coaching work. Many top leadership coaches will insist on a joint meeting with you and your boss to ensure that there are shared expectations about what the challenges and opportunities are, that everyone agrees on how success will be measured, and that the boss is engaged in ensuring effective coaching results.

Role clarity. You need to be clear about what your coach can and cannot do. A leadership coach is an expert on leadership, but you are the only expert on the whole set of challenges and opportunities facing you in your context. Coaching is designed to challenge you to think more deeply, explore alternatives you haven't previously thought enough about, expand your perceptual framework, and create and execute action plans. The great value your coach brings is helping you decide and act more effectively, not thinking or deciding for you.

Using Assessments

The first step toward a successful leadership coaching experience is assessment of the beginning situation, or setting the benchmark. That includes a thorough picture of you as a leader, your preferences and behaviors, and your impact on others. Typically, various methods are used by well-trained coaches to complete the picture and give the raw material for leadership development. Examples include biographical statements or questionnaires, self-report assessment instruments, surveys of others who know you, organizational performance reviews, and interviews with you and others who know you. The purpose of assessment is not diagnosis, but comprehension and understanding of what can make a real difference. You will need to give permission to a professional coach to implement the assessment plan. You can increase the value of information from others who know you if you let them know you would like their candid participation in filling out surveys or talking to your coach.

A thorough assessment ensures that you and your coach don't go down an unprofitable path. Because all of us have our own explanations for why we do what we do, it is easy to give inadequate attention to other viewpoints. The result is that we can tend to justify or defend our behavior when it would be more beneficial to change it. A complete assessment gives the most well-rounded view of you and the environment in which you work. As a result, you are less likely to keep doing what hasn't worked and more likely to explore alternatives that would not immediately occur to you.

Finally, an objective assessment reduces the anxiety you may feel when starting on a change initiative. It is normal to have some thought that you will find out things you didn't know, negative or critical things. Leadership assessment allows you to get an objective snapshot and see your own actions and thinking from a more objective viewpoint. The most common reaction is a sense that change is manageable and doable, and that it can be a way of fulfilling your gifts and talents rather than some radical demand that you be completely different.

A complete assessment gives the most well-rounded view of you and the environment in which you work.

Creating Action Plans and Coaching Meetings

The most effective leadership coaching moves beyond simply reflecting on what is taking place at the moment and builds a body of experiences from which you are drawing the right lessons. However, different coaches will approach the ongoing meetings with different ways of structuring them. You can reasonably expect that your leadership coach has a plan for assisting your development. It should be based on and fed by the comprehensive assessment and lessons from the intersection of the assessment and your ongoing experiences.

A common model of leadership coaching begins with the creation of clear objectives for your development. What will be different in the impact you have in your leadership roles, and who will be able to describe that difference? Your direct reports? Your boss, peers? In this model, your coach will guide you to the description of the changes that you and others will observe, the behaviors you will need to adopt or change, and the behavioral experiments you will undertake to accomplish them.

Another way of describing this approach is that you will be creating a series of experiments in which you will try on new ways of thinking, acting, and speaking. As you try a new behavior, you will record how it affects your own thinking and the responses of others to you. In this way you can continue to examine your own behavior and the thinking that drives it. Many coaching participants are shocked to discover that small changes in how they speak or what they say can have large effects on how they are perceived. Their posture, tone of voice, or attention can result in a difference between their self-perception and the image others have of them. Small, systematic, iterative changes can maximize your leadership impact in ways that working really hard at poorly aimed changes cannot.

In all longer-term leadership coaching engagements there come times when you may feel unclear about where you are, where you are going, or what progress you've made. This is nature's way of ensuring that you do the necessary realigning and retargeting that is the hallmark of all lasting change. Where you intended to go when you set out was based on what you understood at that moment. In good coaching work, what you learn from session to session provides a new view and requires that you recalibrate your objectives. Keeping your boss and other sponsors aware of this growth is essential to keeping their support, and getting their buy-in to changes in ultimate objectives can really help you. It is of greatest importance that feelings you may have that coaching is going nowhere or that you are not getting the value you need are discussed with your coach. These are critical messages that help set up conversations that lead to rapid growth and significant changes.

Along these lines, you and your coach should be recording your action plans between sessions and noting the results of these experiments. At each session you can expect your coach to guide you via questioning to draw the key lessons from these experiments. No matter what the results of these little ventures are, they can never fail because they are intended to create opportunities to learn about your actions and their impact on others. In the process your consciousness of the interpersonal and group dynamics in which you operate will keep growing, and your ability to influence them will also grow. This can be hard work, but there is no other way to accomplish this except to push yourself into action and observe the consequences.

Measuring Results

How will you and your stakeholders know your coaching work was valuable if you do not measure the results? Whether you are paying for your own coaching or your organization is covering the costs, someone should be evaluating the benefits of this work. For that to be meaningful, you and your coach can decide on appropriate metrics at the outset of the engagement. They should incorporate the needs or opportunities that emerge from the assessment process and should be aligned with the intentions of your manager. These measures may change as you and your coach learn more in the process, but it is not appropriate to leave aside the question of metrics altogether. The result of not specifying measures early in the engagement and reviewing them periodically is the temptation to draw the target around the arrow you've shot, making whatever you've done the desired objective. It is frequently pleasant to have an attentive, smart friend with whom you can talk periodically, but that is not a sufficient reason to embark on a leadership coaching relationship. More to the point, it is a waste of the opportunities afforded by leadership coaching.

In some cases you may use some of the same assessments incorporated in the beginning of your work together. That may mean that your boss or other observers are asked about what they have observed with respect to the desired growth. In what ways do they see the goals sought being fulfilled and the effects on others? You and your coach, either together or separately, can interview those key stakeholders again to get a comprehensive picture of the changes accomplished. The final interview will be brief because it can be targeted to the areas selected during the assessment phase.

Some coaches will propose administering a multirater feedback form (360-degree assessment) again to measure changes. CCL research suggests that most 360-degree assessments are not effective in this way because respondents have higher expectations the second time around and apply a different mental rule for how they rate. In addition, reassessment with a 360-degree instrument usually requires a twelve- to eighteen-month interval. An alternative is a 360-degree assessment designed specifically for measuring the impact of developmental activities. A less scientific but still useful approach is to create a brief survey that specifies the areas you want observers to comment on. There are many Web-based platforms that create surveys to which you can invite observers to respond anonymously.

Completing the Coaching Engagement

Even when leadership coaching continues for long periods of time or repeats several times over a long term, you and your coach will be thinking of how to know you have accomplished your objectives and how to conclude the coaching engagement. Open-ended coaching is not uncommon, but it has the danger of devolving into a friend-for-hire relationship or one with too much dependence on the coach. Leadership coaching can be a beneficial resource throughout one's career, but conceptualizing it in episodes can avoid some potential problems. This means a series of coaching conversations based on a clear desire to grow and a context that can help define what kinds of leadership growth will be beneficial.

The key element in concluding a coaching engagement is not what is done: some coaches create elaborate or consistent rituals that mark the event, and others conclude with "Good luck." The key is that this, like the rest of the coaching engagement, is a decision jointly made. It should at least include a review of what you've done and the results. You may have an obligation to report results or evaluate the coaching, and your thoughtful completion is enormously important. You and your coach should be quite clear about your perceptions of the work and its results, and reports either of you make should contain no surprises.

Selecting a Coach

What makes a great leadership coach? The present state of knowledge is based on experience, not science. Here's what years of coaching experience has suggested.

Surprisingly, initial chemistry between the coach and the person being coached does not appear to predict a great coaching experience. Why would this be so? A good coaching relationship balances challenge and support, and when people are anxious about a new relationship, they tend to overvalue support and warmth. While these are necessary attributes of the coaching relationship, they may not be enough. Other characteristics may be more important in predicting the depth and quality of the coaching relationship and the possibility of great outcomes. Is the coach fearless in facing her own foibles and limitations? Is he thoughtful and able to set aside his ego in the service of your growth? Some of these characteristics will only be known to you after time, so they may not help you select a coach.

What about lists of former clients? Would a history of doing work with great companies suggest that a coach is also great? While a list of clients may make you think that others have found the coach useful, it will not tell you either what service was provided or whether it was what you need. Even testimonials from people who have worked with the coach may not give you the information you need about whether this coach will be able to guide you into the growth you seek. The exception to this is found when trusted colleagues make referrals to leadership coaches they know. This is the most-cited reason for choosing a particular leadership coach: he or she was referred by a trusted individual or organization.

Here are some practical things to consider when selecting a leadership coach.

To Whom Is the Coach Accountable?

While there are many outstanding independent coaches, the nature of the coaching relationship requires that a leadership coach have some clear accountability obligations. The main reason this is important is that you are entrusting your coach with information that is critical to your well-being and the well-being of those for whom you are responsible. Individuals are famously poor at self-policing and taking an objective view of their own performance, and coaches are as subject to this aspect of their humanity as anyone. Coaches are not good evaluators of their own quality of work. They need others to whom they report and who share responsibility for quality.

In many cases, the best way to ensure that coaches are subject to regular measurement of their outcomes and supervision of their coaching practice is to engage a coach who belongs to an organization that can guarantee that quality. This will point you to coaches who are employed in a consulting firm or leadership education firm that invests in management of quality. This supervision may be in the form of a manager who reviews quality and who can be informed of concerns about the coaching, but it could also take the form of a peer consultation group. Has this coach been observed by seasoned professionals and selected based on the quality of work done under observation? Does this coach belong to a group whose members meet regularly to discuss their work with due respect for the privacy of their coachees?

What Credentials Matter?

Leadership coaching is an evolving field, and there are not yet globally accepted credentials for coaches. Many training organizations will credential coaches for a variety of training experiences, from a weekend workshop to year-long multiphase programs. The primary difficulty with such programs is that they build their requirements on theoretical models or models drawn from other disciplines (psychotherapy, for example), and the research on what constitutes the necessary preparation for excellent leadership coaching is still in its infancy. Even mature, complex systems of preparation may only be useful for filtering out those who are not persistent, and it is not clear how important persistence is for coaching outcomes. Ultimately, a coaching credential from an independent school or one from a graduate school is most likely to ensure that your coach will not cause harm, but it may not indicate greatness.

Your best strategy for selecting a coach is to use a combination of factors. Important considerations include experience and a record of success in work that is similar to coaching in some important respect. Academic credentials are also important because such success is indicative of capacity for learning and breadth of background. Recommendations from a colleague or HR professional familiar with a coach's work can be quite helpful. Coaching is sufficiently different from other kinds of professional service that the only way to ensure that coaches are doing the right thing is to watch them do it and see what the results are.

> Your best strategy for selecting a coach is to use a combination of factors.

Be cautious with a newly certified coach who has recently hung out a shingle. Former executives may have been terrific leaders, but they may not be good coaches. The habit of telling may lead them to tell you how to be successful rather than assist you in discovering your own success. Newly minted coaches may have great coaching skills, but they may not have enough experience to be useful in the rough-and-tumble real world of organizational life. You may have to be prepared to help them develop, but it could be a worthy trade-off if you are able to find the right person.

Sources for Leadership Coaches

Firms with Coaches	Regional Boutiques	Individuals by Referral
Safest bet 1. The firm may guarantee the work of the coach. 2. If the fit is not good, the firm can supply another coach. 3. Assurance can be costly. 4. There is existing quality management. 5. You should ask how coaches are recruited, selected, trained, certified, and managed.	May have local references 1. Coaches may have peers to whom they are accountable. 2. Peer supervision may be used. 3. Boutiques are sometimes slightly less expensive than firms.	May have widely varying experience 1. Coaches may have a wide range of fees. 2. They may have no backup and little support. 3. A personal referral is the best source.

A leadership coach can help you keep the focus in the right place in the moment.

Questions for Prospective Leadership Coaches

1. **Besides your clients, to whom are you accountable for your work?**

   You're looking for some indication that they have arranged for their own professional growth through reflection on what they are doing.

2. **If you get into a coaching situation in which you are not sure what to do or say, what would you do?**

   You're looking for some information that would tell you that they recognize limits to their expertise. Will they bring it up to you that they are stumped or pretend expertise they don't have? Do they have external resources they can call on for help in thinking through what they are doing?

3. **Tell me about a recent successful coaching engagement. What did you do? What did the person being coached do to contribute to the success?**

   You're looking for evidence that they have a systematic model in their minds about their own actions. You're seeking an awareness that the coaching relationship is a collaboration in which each person contributes to the growth.

Are You Ready?

It may seem odd to end this guidebook with a discussion of your readiness for coaching, but readiness is not a static state based on how you feel about coaching. *Readiness* is a term used to describe your awareness of what you bring to the coaching engagement. It cannot be measured in binary terms—that is, either ready or not ready. In fact, whether you're ready or not, leadership coaching can be a powerful means of achieving your full potential as a leader in all parts of your life. However, the more thought you have given to understanding what you bring to the coaching relationship, the more effective you will be as a partner in creating an optimal leadership coaching process. The following questions are designed to help you think about your readiness in such a way that you can be as helpful as possible to your leadership coach as he or she guides you through this period of accelerated growth.

Defining your context or situation	
1. Do you see a need for development (problems, bored, worried, eager)? 2. Does someone else see a need (your boss, HR) or want to give you an opportunity?	Use this information to start aligning your perceptions with those of others. Recognize that nothing is really only personal and that there is a social and organizational context that will affect your success with coaching.
Describing your motivation	
1. What is your motivation to change? 2. Do you have to increase support of your boss or others? 3. Are you worried about your possibilities? 4. Do you not know what to do next?	Tracking changes in what motivates you and the level of enthusiasm or lack of it can help determine what steps will be necessary to maximize the benefits from the work.

Understanding your learning style	
1. Do you learn best from your conversations with others? 2. Do you get the most from a clear structure and complete, accurate information? 3. Do you learn best from trying different behaviors and seeing how they turn out? 4. Do you need the big picture, how it all fits together, before you get to the details?	Your learning style helps determine the best approaches for development and can reduce the chance that you are wasting effort and time trying to copy someone else's approach.
Understanding your ability to use relationships for growth	
1. How does accountability matter in your persistence? 2. Does support help you stay motivated, or does it let you relax and slack off?	Sometimes accountability has a paradoxical effect: knowing you will need to share your progress with someone can breed resentment rather than enthusiasm. How does the involvement of others in your plans affect you?

If you believe that leadership coaching is a promising avenue for your development at this time, the next step is a conversation with your internal advocate. You may want to explore options for your growth and how coaching can be a significant accelerator for it.

Suggested Readings

Hart, E. W., & Kirkland, K. (2001). *Using your executive coach.* Greensboro, NC: Center for Creative Leadership.

Kirkland, K., & Manoogian, S. (1998). *Ongoing feedback: How to get it, how to use it.* Greensboro, NC: Center for Creative Leadership.

McCauley, C. D. (2006). *Developmental assignments: Creating learning experiences without changing jobs.* Greensboro, NC: Center for Creative Leadership.

Ting, S., & Scisco, P. (Eds.). (2006). *The CCL handbook of coaching: A guide for the leader coach.* San Francisco: Jossey-Bass.

Background

The Center for Creative Leadership has been coaching leaders for over thirty years. We coach and teach others to coach because of our commitment to leadership development. We see coaching not only as an essential component of that learning process but also as an essential capability of good leaders and leadership.

We regard coaching as one way to facilitate learning. As a process, it is highly compatible with CCL's mission to improve leadership for society and the world and with its philosophy of development. This philosophy contains the principles that (1) leadership can be learned, and experiences offer us opportunities to learn the lessons of leadership, and (2) understanding how others see us and our impact on them allows us to make choices on what and how to change and adapt.

Over the years, CCL has built a coaching framework based on its knowledge and practice of leadership development that we believe underpins any good leadership coaching initiative:

- relationship: the context within which the coaching occurs

- assessment, challenge, and support: the core elements of CCL's leader development model

- results: the direct and indirect outcomes of the coaching process

CCL has integrated its coaching as a practice with other learning experiences and developmental processes. While we support the use of coaching as a stand-alone experience, and there are times when that may be the preferred development experience, our practice is consistent with our belief that a variety of learning experiences offers the greatest likelihood for success.

Our work involving the practice of coaching now spans a wide range. We offer stand-alone coaching work with top executives to midlevel executives that includes intensive assessment and development planning conducted in concert with internal HR processes. We have begun to establish practice norms for team coaching. We are involved with helping leaders, coaches, and HR professionals improve their coaching skills. We also integrate coaching with other learning experiences such as action learning projects and classroom-based learning.

Key Point Summary

Leadership coaching is a formal engagement in which a qualified coach works with an organizational leader in a series of dynamic, private sessions designed to establish and achieve clear goals that will result in improved business effectiveness for the individual, as well as his or her team and organization. It is not the right solution for every kind of growth or development, but some situations seem ideally suited to this approach, including increased complexity, organizational expectations, demands for behavior change, significant transitions, predicted changes, highly politicized environments, and moves from a tactical to a strategic role. It is often most effective when combined with other learning resources, such as leadership development programs, mentoring, feedback, developmental assignments, colleagues, and psychotherapy.

Every coaching engagement is unique, but there are consistent elements of the coaching experience: setting up the coaching engagement (boundaries, organizational expectations, role clarity), using assessments, creating action plans and coaching meetings, measuring results, and completing the coaching engagement.

Your best strategy for selecting a coach is to use a combination of factors. Important considerations include experience and a record of success in work that is similar to coaching in some important respect. Academic credentials are also important because such success is indicative of capacity for learning and breadth of background. Recommendations from a colleague or HR professional familiar with a coach's work can be quite helpful.

The more thought you have given to understanding what you bring to the coaching relationship, the more effective you will be as a partner in creating an optimal leadership coaching process. Think about your situation, motivation, learning style, and ability to use relationships for growth. If you believe that leadership coaching is a promising avenue for your development at this time, the next step is a conversation with your internal advocate. You may want to explore options for your growth and how coaching can be a significant accelerator for it.

Ordering Information

TO GET MORE INFORMATION, TO ORDER OTHER IDEAS INTO ACTION GUIDEBOOKS, OR TO FIND OUT ABOUT BULK-ORDER DISCOUNTS, PLEASE CONTACT US BY PHONE AT 336-545-2810 OR VISIT OUR ONLINE BOOKSTORE AT WWW.CCL.ORG/GUIDEBOOKS.

CPSIA information can be obtained
at www.ICGtesting.com
Printed in the USA
BVOW07s1039050416

442939BV00005BA/9/P

9 781604 910438